HOW TO PASS
THE CPA EXAMS

WITH SCORES IN THE 90s!

◆ ◆ ◆

MIKAYLA HUTCHINGS

CONTENTS

INTRODUCTION

"Nothing is impossible. The
word itself says 'I'm possible.'"
– Audrey Hepburn

Study material: $3,393
Exam fees: $1,079
Starbucks coffee: $476
Passing all of the exams with scores in the 90s: Priceless

I am not going to lie to you. The CPA exams will test your limits, as well as your patience. The process can seem never-ending at times and, quite honestly, a major pain in the butt. However, do not let yourself give up! It will be worth it in the end - trust me. Keep reminding yourself of the reasons why you started studying in the first place and how it will feel once you are officially done. More importantly, remember that the exams are NOT impossible! In fact, studying for the exams can become quite manageable once you learn how to study more effectively and efficiently. The way I studied led me to scores in the 90s; therefore, I felt the need to share my experiences and study methods with the world in hopes that others can have that same "priceless" experience.

I strongly believe that if you study like I did, and put in the appropriate amount of time, you will walk out of the exams feeling somewhat confident. Note: I said "somewhat" and not "completely" confident. There is no way to walk out of the exam knowing your exact score; however, being "somewhat confident" is a heck of a lot better than feeling like you bombed it. Agreed? Cool - let's move on.

Before I get into my advice on how to pass the CPA exams, I would like to take the time to introduce myself. I am hoping this part provides some validity to my claims that I can help you score in the 90s. My name is Mikayla, and I am officially DONE with the CPA exams! I have one month before I start as an Audit Assistant at a Big 4 firm, so I have decided to take this time to share any insight that I possibly can to help YOU pass, too! I studied from December 2018 - July 2019 and received the following scores:

Regulation (REG) - 95
Business Environment and Concepts (BEC) - 94
Financial Accounting and Reporting (FAR) - 90
Auditing and Attestation (AUD) - 92

In May 2018, I graduated from John Carroll University in Cleveland, Ohio with a BSBA in Accountancy and a minor in Entrepreneurship. Right after undergrad, I started working toward an MBA at John Carroll in order to get 150 credits to sit for the exams (rules vary by state, but in Ohio, you need 150 credits before you can even apply to take the exams). I reached 150 credits in December 2018, so I immediately applied for my NTS (Notice to Schedule) and started studying for the exams right away. Each state has a different application process, but my application through NASBA (National Association of State Boards of Accountancy) took approximately 4 weeks to be approved. I completed REG and BEC while in the MBA program, and FAR and AUD after my May 2019 graduation. Completing two exams while in school was one of the best decisions I have ever made. I now have one month to relax before I start work, or in my case, write a book! My worst fear was having to study after a full work day at a Big 4 firm, so I wanted to get the exams done before I started work in September. It obviously wouldn't have been the end of the world; but, if you have the chance, why not try? As soon as you have enough credits, do NOT hesitate to start the process! I'm sure those people working and studying full-time would agree with me.

I ended up studying about 8 weeks for FAR and REG and 6 weeks for AUD and BEC. I understand that many people try cutting this time frame in half in order to cram the exams into one summer - and I know this is certainly possible! However, if you are able to give yourself more time, I honestly think that it is worth it. Because I gave myself more time, I could learn at a more manageable pace and say "yes" to more opportunities over the course of 7 months. Whether it be dinner with my family or a night out downtown with my friends, I was able to take those needed breaks to recharge instead of studying 24/7. I realize the amount of time needed to study may vary per person, but I felt that 6-8 weeks was perfect for me to truly understand the material enough without ever feeling crunched for time.

In terms of study material, my employer suggested and provided reimbursement for the Becker program. Therefore, I solely used Becker and didn't necessarily research other options. Becker is supposedly the best program, but I don't have any personal experience to back that statement up other than my high scores. I have always been curious if I would have received the same scores using another program; but, regardless, my experience with Becker was nothing short of excellent. I thought the software provided a considerable amount of tools to help me learn the information, and most importantly, a large variety of resources that could be adapted to any learning style. When I took each exam, I recognized every single topic from the Becker material and it was up to me to apply the information I was taught. If you are in the process of choosing a study program because your firm does not provide reimbursement, I highly recommend Becker and think it is certainly worth the investment (I mean, it led to pretty high scores for myself and a lot of my peers...). Throughout the rest of the book, my study methods will inevitably be based on how Becker is structured. However, I strongly believe that my tips could be adjusted to any study program. In addition, I will be providing advice on aspects beyond the study material, such as how to approach the exam itself, so definitely keep reading even if you have chosen another review program!

Everyone learns in a different way and at a different pace. That being said, I recognize that my study methods may not apply to every single reader. However, do yourself a favor and keep an open mind. You might surprise yourself by considering a study approach that you have never thought to implement before. Do I expect you to follow every single piece of advice that I give? Of course not. I simply want this book to be a reflection of my own personal journey and how it led me to scores in the 90s. Even if just a couple of my tips help you receive passing scores, I would call this book a success!

Disclaimer: If you knew me in college, you would know that I was always the "go-to" person for homework help, class projects, or the most epic study guides. I graduated top of my accounting class at John Carroll, and I had a GPA of 3.99 (shoutout to Dr. Bloom in Intermediate Accounting for giving me that A-). However, the LAST thing I want you to takeaway is that you can't score in the 90s just because you aren't as "smart" as me. That is far from the truth. The key to the CPA exams is to understand HOW to study and then put in the appropriate amount of time, as opposed to your prior accounting knowledge. That being said, I believe I am one of the most qualified individuals to teach you how to study for 2 simple reasons: 1) my 3.99 GPA in college reflects that I have already mastered how to appropriately study and 2) a very small percentage of candidates pass all four exams on the first try; yet, I did... with each score in the 90s. I am not in any way trying to boast; I am trying to prove why you should trust me to guide you through studying for the CPA exams. I believe my intelligence helped me realize what the best ways to study were and how to approach certain exam questions, which is what I hope to share with you throughout this book. BUT, I had to put in the time - just like everyone else.

EXAM STRUCTURE

*"You have to learn the rules of
the game. And then you have
to play better than anyone
else." –Albert Einstein*

For those of you at the beginning stages of the CPA exam process, I think it is crucial for you to understand how the exams are structured before I start discussing my study methods. That being said, if you already know the format and content of each exam, then feel free to just skim over this chapter.

There are four exams (and I took them in the following order): Regulation (REG), Business Environment and Concepts (BEC), Financial Accounting and Reporting (FAR), and Auditing and Attestation (AUD). You can take the exams in any order that you want. FAR and REG are supposedly the "harder" of the four, while BEC and AUD are supposedly the "easier" ones. I think they just got these designations because FAR and REG consist of more units, and therefore more content, in the Becker textbooks. When deciding what order to take the exams, I decided to do "hard, easy, hard, easy." There are so many different combinations you could do, and I have heard several explanations of why you should do them in a certain order. All in all, it is up to you and what you think makes most sense. I personally liked the order that I took the exams. If I were to give any opinion, it would be to take AUD last because I found it to be easiest to study for (and trust me, my motivation went downhill during each exam, so it was nice not having to focus as much on my last one). Also, I found that taking FAR before AUD helped tremendously since auditing is all about analyzing financial statement information, which you learn about in FAR.

You need a 75 to pass. I know... it looks like I went overboard with scores in the 90s. But, honestly, I think it is best to aim high. There is no way to even guess what score you will receive because, theoretically, the AICPA could decide to throw out the questions you nailed and grade the questions you were unsure about. Yeah, that's right. There are such things as "pretest questions," which are questions the AICPA uses "to collect data." Of course, you don't know which questions are real or pretest, which adds to the uncertainty of how the exams are ultimately graded. Speaking of uncertainty, the AICPA uses a "multistage adaptive test delivery model" (whatever that means...). Essentially, the testlets will get more difficult as you answer more questions correctly; however, to make it "fair," difficult questions are weighted higher. Nevertheless, it is not worth your time trying to figure out the confusing grading process - just focus on following my advice and you will be perfectly fine.

Most of the tests consist of Multiple Choice Questions (MCQs) and Task-Based Simulations (TBSs). I will be using those acronyms from now on, so take note now! MCQs are pretty self-explanatory; these questions consist of four answer choices that you have to choose from. TBSs, on the other hand, are designed to simulate real-life scenarios. The possible types of TBSs are endless, and you will get more familiar with them within the Becker software. They could range from doing calculations and entering the correct answer as a number, selecting answers from a drop-down, analyzing attachments to come to a "yes/no" answer, or entering a journal entry. One TBS will always be an Authoritative Literature (AL) question (with the exception of BEC). I will cover how to approach AL questions later, but long story short, you have to sort through accounting standards to find the correct guidance to answer the question being asked (these questions are a blessing - trust me). You can actually use the AL to help with any TBS, aside from the designated AL questions, so it is extremely beneficial to practice navigating the standards in your free time.

You have 4 hours to complete each exam, and each exam consists of 5 testlets. Managing your time during the exam is crucial. On exam day, as soon as you sit down at your desk, I recommend writing times in the corner of your dry-erase board to signal when you should be moving on to each respective testlet. I think writing down times kept me accountable and forced me to move on from testlets I wasn't making progress on. When I discuss how each exam is structured, I will share with you what times I wrote down on my board to stay on track. I will also mention this strategy again when discussing how to approach the exam on exam day.

I obviously cannot disclose any specific questions and/or answers from my exams. Therefore, I will talk very generally about each exam throughout this book. I will dedicate a whole chapter to approaching the exam on exam day, but here is the basic content and structure of REG, BEC, FAR, and AUD for you "newbies." This information can be found on the AICPA website, as well as through your study program.

Regulation (REG)
According to the AICPA (effective July 1, 2019), REG allocates its content accordingly: Ethics, Professional Responsibilities and Federal Tax Procedures: 10-20%; Business Law: 10-20%; Federal Taxation of Property Transactions: 12-22%; Federal Taxation of Individuals: 15-25%; and
Federal Taxation of Entities: 28-38%.

The exam consists of 5 testlets, and I budgeted the following amount of time:

Testlet 1: 38 MCQs [spend 40 minutes - move on at 3:20]
Testlet 2: 38 MCQs [spend 40 minutes - move on at 2:40]
Testlet 3: 2 TBSs [spend 40 minutes - move on at 2:00]
[Standard 15 minute break]
Testlet 4: 3 TBSs [spend 60 minutes - move on at 1:00]
Testlet 5: 3 TBSs [spend 60 minutes]

Business Environment and Concepts (BEC)

According to the AICPA (effective July 1, 2019), BEC allocates its content accordingly: Corporate Governance: 17-27%; Economic Concepts and Analysis: 17-27%; Financial Management: 11-21%; Information Technology: 15-25%; and Operations Management: 15-25%.

BEC is a little different from the other exams because there is actually a writing portion (*insert groan here*). I don't know why I dreaded the Written Communications Tasks (WCTs) so much. I've heard that "as long as you know English, you're fine." I was just intimidated by having to write in a pressured situation, especially if I wasn't comfortable with the topic being asked. Essentially, you have to read a scenario and then construct a professional document in response, whether it be a letter, memo, or other form of writing. In my opinion, WCTs aren't necessarily hard; they are just annoying. I will talk about how to approach the written portion later on and will just focus on the structure of the exam now.

The exam consists of 5 testlets, and I budgeted the following amount of time:

Testlet 1: 31 MCQs [spend 40 minutes - move on at 3:20]
Testlet 2: 31 MCQs [spend 40 minutes - move on at 2:40]
Testlet 3: 2 TBSs [spend 40 minutes - move on at 2:00]
[Standard 15 minute break]
Testlet 4: 2 TBSs [spend 40 minutes - move on at 1:20]

<u>Testlet 5:</u> 3 WCTs [spend 80 minutes]

Financial Accounting and Reporting (FAR)

According to the AICPA (effective July 1, 2019), FAR allocates its content accordingly: Conceptual Framework, Standard-Setting and Financial Reporting: 25-35%; Select Financial Statement Accounts: 30-40%; Select Transactions: 20-30%; and State and Local Governments: 5-15%.

The exam consists of 5 testlets, and I budgeted the following amount of time:
<u>Testlet 1:</u> 33 MCQs [spend 40 minutes - move on at 3:20]
<u>Testlet 2:</u> 33 MCQs [spend 40 minutes - move on at 2:40]
<u>Testlet 3:</u> 2 TBSs [spend 40 minutes - move on at 2:00]
[Standard 15 minute break]
<u>Testlet 4:</u> 3 TBSs [spend 60 minutes - move on at 1:00]
<u>Testlet 5:</u> 3 TBSs [spend 60 minutes]

Auditing and Attestation (AUD)

According to the AICPA (effective July 1, 2019), AUD allocates its content accordingly: Ethics, Professional Responsibilities and General Principles: 15-25%; Assessing Risk and Developing a Planned Response: 20-30%; Performing Further Procedures and Obtaining Evidence: 30-40%; and Forming Conclusions and Reporting: 15-25%.

The exam consists of 5 testlets, and I budgeted the following amount of time:
<u>Testlet 1:</u> 36 MCQs [spend 40 minutes - move on at 3:20]
<u>Testlet 2:</u> 36 MCQs [spend 40 minutes - move on at 2:40]
<u>Testlet 3:</u> 2 TBSs [spend 40 minutes - move on at 2:00]
[Standard 15 minute break]
<u>Testlet 4:</u> 3 TBSs [spend 60 minutes - move on at 1:00]
<u>Testlet 5:</u> 3 TBSs [spend 60 minutes]

STUDY METHOD #1:
STICK TO A SCHEDULE

"A goal without a plan is just a wish." – Antoine de Saint-Exupéry

Hallelujah! We are FINALLY getting to the secrets of my success. Thanks for hanging in there; I just felt it was necessary that you understand how each exam is structured before I outline how you should study for them. Anyways, I would argue that sticking to a schedule is probably the most important part of passing the CPA exams. You may be thinking, "Really Mikayla? I could have told you that one." However, I know a lot of people that "studied at their own pace" and would "take it when they are ready." More often than not, those attitudes led to procrastination and failing scores.

First and foremost, you NEED to create a schedule outlining when you want to take each exam. This is SO important. Having a date in mind truly keeps you accountable throughout the entire process. If you do not make a schedule, you are prone to delaying test dates because "you don't feel ready yet." Delaying one test date will inevitably delay the rest. Before you know it, the rough timeline you envisioned in your head has instantly doubled. I guarantee that you will not want to extend the studying process any longer than you have to. If you are to remember any piece of advice from this book, remember this: WRITE DOWN YOUR SCHED-ULE. It is a proven fact, folks! You are more likely to accomplish your goals if you write them down. Keep yourself accountable.

I created my exam schedule several months before I even started studying (*nerd alert*). I stuck to the schedule almost exactly, give or take a few days. The Prometric testing center may not have the dates available to accommodate your exact schedule, so you may need to compromise. However, try your best to stick to it as closely as you can. By having that schedule in mind (and written out!), you will be much more likely to push through those long days of studying in order to stay on track.

When creating my exam schedule, I took Becker's Live Online classes into consideration, as well as "blackout" months. I will explain both of those factors below. Additionally, I took my personal life into consideration. For instance, I left the most time to review for FAR since finals week, my birthday, and a short trip to Florida all fell within that time frame. Anyways, as you can see below, I typically left 3 weeks to review after finishing my last Live Online class. As an example, here is the exact schedule I followed:

REG: Live Online: Jan. 5 - Jan. 26 (Sat.) -- take exam Feb. 13
BEC: Live Online: Feb. 23 - Mar. 9 (Sat.) -- take exam Apr. 1
FAR: Live Online: Apr. 6 - May 4 (Sat.) -- take exam May 31
AUD: Live Online: June 3 - June 20 (M./Th.) -- take exam July 18

As I mentioned earlier, make sure to plan your test dates around the "blackout" periods. At the end of every quarter, there is a certain amount of time where you cannot sit for any exam. For instance, in 2019, the blackout periods are in March, June, September, and December from the 11th to the end of each month. Also, keep in mind that you have to pass all four exams in a rolling 18-month period. This 18-month time frame begins on the date you pass your first section. Because the countdown begins once you pass your first test, many online forums recommend you take a tougher exam, like FAR, first. If you take a harder exam first and happen to fail, it's not a huge deal because your 18-month count-down hasn't started yet. However, if you are struggling to pass your last test and the time runs out, you have to start over... (Dun, dun, dunnn...). All in all, you don't need to worry about this if you follow my study methods and commit yourself to studying for a predetermined amount of time. I passed in 7 months very com-fortably, and I know several people who have passed in 4 months. Don't give up!

As you can see, I also planned the timing of my tests around when Becker's Live Online classes were being offered. Live Online classes are provided by Becker aside from the normal study pro-gram. These classes are taught by a live instructor through a webi-nar software. The instructors would typically go through the Becker textbook, page by page, and teach the information in their own unique way. Sometimes, the instructors would even create their own study guides and walk us through them. For my first 3 exams, I signed up for the 6-hour Saturday classes; however, there are also 3-hour weekday options (I did Mon./Thurs. for AUD). The instructor would cover 2 units per class (1 unit if it is a weekday class), and you were supposed to complete the "homework" for those units in the Becker software the following week (skills practices, MCQs, TBSs...). However, I found it WAY more benefi-cial to do the "homework" BEFORE class. This made the Live On-line classes a great review tool for me. Since I was hearing the les-sons for a second time, I was able to focus on what the instructor was actually saying rather than busily writing down notes. The webinar even had a tool where you could submit your questions during the class and a licensed CPA would respond right away. Since I had already had a week to process the information by com-pleting the "homework" before class, I felt that I could better for-mulate questions during the class. Surprisingly, after talking to several of my accounting peers, many did not utilize the Live On-line classes. I was shocked because the classes: 1) kept me accountable by encouraging me to have a set number of lessons done before each class and 2) encouraged me to review what I had already learned in the Becker software, which helped me understand the material on a deeper level.

As I spoke about briefly in the introduction, I studied about 8 weeks for FAR and REG and 6 weeks for AUD and BEC. To be completely honest, I gave myself this amount of time because the Live Online classes happened to line up that way. However, I think the timing ended up working out perfectly. Roughly speaking, I probably studied between 6-8 hours per day. However, there were definitely some days where I only studied a couple hours, if that. If you want to get the tests done in a shorter amount of time, you would obviously have to sacrifice more hours per day to study. Or maybe you wouldn't - it's hard to judge. I don't think there is an exact answer to how many hours you should study for each exam. Everybody is different. I am just stating what worked for me and led to my high scores. All in all, if you have the luxury of spacing the exams out like I did over 6-7 months, I personally believe that you will have a higher chance of passing and will experience less stress induced by time constraints.

Now that you know when you want to take each exam (and have it written down!), you need to plan out how you will utilize your time each week. Since I took the Live Online classes, I knew I had to get 2 units done per week. This would then leave me with about 3 weeks to review for each test. At the beginning of each week, I would create a schedule of what I wanted to get done each day and wouldn't leave the library until it was done. As you already know, my typical goal was to get 2 units done by the end of the week. Let's say that 2 units had 12 modules combined. If I went to the library every day from Sunday - Friday, I would typically plan to do 2 modules per day. On the other hand, let's assume that I had a family event on Sunday and wanted to hang out with my friends on Friday. I could also choose to do 3 modules per day from Monday - Thursday. Whatever the situation was, I would make it work and have a written plan going into each week in order to reach my end goal.

To prove how important scheduling is, I have a quick story for you to close out this chapter. I always chose to study in the John Carroll library because I enjoyed catching up with my accounting peers who were also studying for the exams. Each week, I would always check in with one particular classmate because he regularly sat at the table next to mine. Whenever I would ask him how it was going, it would be the same story, "I'm still studying for FAR…" By the time I got to FAR myself in April (with 2 other tests already passed), he was STILL studying for it! One day, he even jokingly said, "Mikayla, you need to slow down!" It's not like I was taking the exams extremely fast (many of my peers take them in half the time); I was just sticking to the schedule I made. I started to ask some questions to understand why he hadn't gotten through the material yet, and his answers revolved around wanting to go at his own pace. He was shocked when I said that I get through 2 units per week. I tried to explain that even though I get through the information pretty fast on my first go-around, I am able to learn the material for a second time through the Live Online class, and multiple other times during the long review period I leave at the end. I recently found out that he didn't take FAR until July! I think it would be nearly impossible to remember something that you learned months ago, so I definitely think there is such thing as "too long" of a study period. Because he "wanted to go at his own pace," he took nearly 7 months to study for an exam. I passed all 4 exams before he even took his first one. Don't make this process miserable for yourself. Stick to a schedule, take the tests when you had planned to, and move on with your life!

STUDY METHOD #2: HOW TO BEST UTILIZE BECKER

"The secret of success is to do the common things uncommonly well." – John D. Rockefeller

Becker provides you with the tools to succeed. It is up to YOU to use them effectively and efficiently. I am going to use this chapter to discuss exactly how I would study for an exam using Becker. Since I already touched on how the Live Online classes work, I am just going to focus on the software itself.

Becker is split up by units, which is further split up by modules. Each module consists of a lecture, skills practice, and MCQs. At the end of each unit, TBSs are provided to help you practice applying the information you just learned. I completed 100% of these tasks to prepare for each exam. I realize that each exam consists of different content, so it is valid to consider changing your study routine depending on the type of information you have to learn; however, I would never skip out on one of Becker's "homework" assignments. I completed each task no matter what exam I was studying for. Instead, I would change my review process for each exam to better reflect the type of material being tested. I will talk about how to review in the next chapter, so stay tuned!

Note: I realize that there are other study providers besides Becker. However, I am sure that the other programs are set up similarly and that you can still take away a few study tips from this chapter.

Lecture

The pre-recorded lectures can vary anywhere between 10 minutes to over an hour. My #1 tip for lectures: watch them at a faster speed. In the bottom left-hand corner, there is a settings icon where you can adjust the speed to 1.25, 1.50, etc... (each instructor talks at a different speed, so you have to adjust accordingly). This tip helped me get through lectures at a much more desirable speed since I can't stand when people talk slow... (I can't be the only one). Plus, it meant that I could be done faster! Score!

During the lecture, the instructor will underline certain phrases, as well as write down key points. I recommend writing down the same exact notations into your physical textbook. Hearing the information and then immediately writing it down will help you better recall the concepts in the future.

I have heard that some people like to read the module and take their own notes before, or even instead of, listening to the lecture. In my opinion... don't waste your time. The instructor will walk through everything you need to know with helpful notations and mnemonics. Therefore, I strongly recommend using the pre-recorded lecture as your first time learning the information. Reading the book would just take up valuable time that you could have spent elsewhere, especially when you aren't sure which concepts to focus your time on. I understand that reading on your own first may help you get familiarized with the topics, but I think the lectures do a better job at helping you grasp the larger concepts in a more time-efficient manner. On the other hand, I am a huge advocate of reading the book as you review. During the review process, you should be mastering those finer details, so reading the textbook makes sense.

Skills Practice
Skills practices are provided to help you review and apply the information that you just learned in the lecture. A typical skills practice consists of a video summarizing key points in the lecture, as well as a couple exercises. Even though I found skills practices to be a little redundant and annoying (you will undoubtedly get sick of the instructors' "humor..."), I still made an effort to complete all of them. No matter how pointless you think they are, I would not recommend skipping them because you may learn something new! There were multiple times where a topic was covered much more in depth in a skills practice than the lecture itself. If a resource is there to help you learn and pass the exam, then use it!

On a side note, I will admit that I started to get lazy with the exercises. Instead of trying to complete the exercises myself without "cheating" by looking at the answers, I began to just watch the videos explaining the solution. I still think this is an effective way to learn as you can see how a professional approaches the questions. If you don't want to waste time on answering the questions yourself, then my advice would be to at least watch the solution videos. Get your money's worth out of Becker - don't skip the skills practices!

Multiple Choice Questions (MCQs)
Practicing multiple choice questions is EXTREMELY important. First, since 50% of the exams consist of MCQs, you will get exposure to the types of questions that will be asked on the actual exam. Second, MCQs help you learn the material in a different form than simply reading the book. By having to choose between certain answer choices, you are proving to yourself that you actually understand the information.

My biggest tip when working on MCQs is to understand WHY you got a question right or wrong. Becker does a great job of explaining why a certain answer is correct AND why the other answer choices are wrong. READ THESE EXPLANATIONS. You might learn something else about the topic that you didn't already know! By understanding instead of memorizing answers to MCQs, you will inevitably learn more and be able to apply this knowledge to a larger set of potential questions dealing with that topic going forward.

On various online forums, I always see people asking others what their average MCQ score is. I would argue that it doesn't even matter. As long are you are reading the explanations as you go and understanding the information, who cares if you get 50% or 75% of the questions right? If you are dying to know, I typically ranged between 70%-90% on my first attempt. But again, I don't think it matters as long as you are learning and absorbing the information. Just because you didn't know an MCQ the first time, doesn't mean that you won't know it during the actual exam. Study tip: learn from your mistakes!

Speaking of learning from your mistakes, write your mistakes down! I think this study method is extremely helpful, and, ironically, I don't know anyone else who has done this! For every exam, I had a notebook that I used to write down explanations of why I missed certain questions. Since I didn't want to waste time writing down every question, answer, and explanation, I would simply just write a bullet point outlining the accounting concept I was unaware of when I answered the question incorrectly. By doing this, I would very rarely make that same mistake again. Who cares how many mistakes you make in the beginning stages of studying? Who cares what your average MCQ score is? As long as you are grasping the concepts and understand the information in time for the exam, that's all that matters.

On a side note, I also utilized https://www.cpareviewforfree.com for additional MCQ practice. I know some candidates decide to pay for supplementary MCQs through other study programs; however, this website is FREE and has more than enough practice questions. I do not think it is necessary to seek study material beyond Becker; however, it was reassuring to know that I was exposed to more than one source for exam review (and could answer those questions just as well as Becker's). Plus, any practice is worthwhile, especially when you need help with one particular area.

Task-Based Simulations (TBSs)
Now that you have completed each module's lecture, skills practice, and MCQs, it is time to tackle the TBSs. As I have covered briefly, task-based simulations can come in a variety of different formats. For instance, you may have to sort through several attachments and come to some conclusion (whether that be a 'yes/no' response, calculated number, journal entry, or an answer via a drop-down). You may have to calculate a variety of ratios and analyze why the ratios went up or down. You may even have to fill out a financial statement. The possibilities are endless. Honestly, it may sound confusing now, but you will get used to the possible TBS formats as you practice them in Becker. The TBS questions provided in Becker are set up similarly to the ones in the actual exam so that there are no "surprises" on exam day.

During a TBS, you are given access to an online calculator and Excel. The online calculator that they provide in Becker is very similar to the one that the actual exam provides. On the other hand, Becker's Excel is not an accurate representation of what you will see on exam day. Becker's Excel isn't even Excel... I don't even know how to describe it. I tried to figure it out for 10 minutes one day and decided it wasn't worth my time. However, the actual exam will give you access to a much more functional Excel to use (hallelujah!). In fact, I would recommend just opening the actual Excel program on your computer when practicing

TBSs since it is much more realistic to the one provided on exam day.

TBSs also provide you with an Authoritative Literature (AL) to use. There are several sources within the AL, such as the AICPA Professional Standards (used for AUD), PCAOB Auditing Standards (used for AUD), Internal Revenue Code (used for REG), and the FASB Codification (used for FAR). Exactly one TBS on each exam (with the exception of BEC) will be an AL question. I guarantee that you will look forward to these. Long story short, you are given an accounting scenario that ends in a question. You have to answer the question by citing the correct standard that references the answer. These questions generally took me around 5 minutes to answer, so I was always able to use that extra allotted time on more difficult TBSs in my exam. The AL intimidated me at first, but you will get used to how to navigate it after practicing the AL questions in Becker. My best advice would be to practice using the "Advanced Search" feature and getting good at determining what keywords to use. Study tip: when you are tired of studying all day, a mindless (yet beneficial) activity would be to sort through the AL by just clicking on random topics. See where it ends up taking you. Being familiar with the AL can save you a lot of valuable time on exam day.

As you practice TBSs in the Becker software, there are two different ways of displaying the correct answers. First, there is the written solution. This is helpful if you are already confident about how to get to the answer and just want to check your work. The written solution not only has the correct answers, but it also has a quick explanation of how to solve it. On the other hand, if you need a bit more guidance on how to approach the TBS, there are also "SkillMaster videos." These videos walk you through how to attempt the TBS from start to finish. I loved these videos and appreciated the instructors' advice on how to approach certain questions, especially when I had no idea where to begin.

I want to be completely honest with all of you. I HATED practicing TBSs. I dreaded them! The amount of time and energy it took to complete them was a giant pain in my butt. However, we ended up having a love-hate relationship. Even though they can be annoying, you end up learning SO MUCH from them. Just one TBS can apply several different accounting principles. Also, by completing the TBSs, I not only became more familiar with what a possible exam question could be like, but I also learned how to take information from a textbook and apply it to certain scenarios. By doing that, I learned the information through understanding rather than memory and could better recall the information on exam day!

While studying for the exams, I will openly admit that I read CPA forums for fun to see how other people were studying (I know... I'm a nerd... but I guess you are too for reading this book). I continually saw people say, "skip the TBSs and just focus on MCQs all day every day." I also heard this same advice from my peers. My response: I disagree, but I understand the thought process behind these comments. I accept the fact that you can get more out of practicing MCQs due to the ability to crank out tons of questions dealing with various topics in one sitting. Practicing MCQs is a great way to learn information in a fast-paced and repetitive way. I get it. And quite honestly, if I was more crunched for time, I think TBSs would be one of the first things I eliminate from my study schedule in order to solely focus on MCQs. However, if you have the time, and want a greater chance of receiving a high score, do yourself a favor and attempt all of the TBSs. It can't possibly hurt. In fact, I think becoming more familiar with how to approach TBSs is what bumped me up to scores in the 90s. Being able to memorize an MCQ is one thing, but being able to recall that information and apply it to a TBS is a whole different ball game that will help you immensely on exam day.

Flashcards
In my (unpopular) opinion, skip the flashcards... I think you can

review more effectively by simply reading the textbook. A lot of my accounting peers swore by Becker's flashcards; however, I did not understand the benefit. I get that it is easy to flip through flashcards if you are on the couch and what not, but I think it is just as easy to flip through your book (or in my case, I liked to scroll through the pre-annotated book online). The flashcards just seemed vague to me and not worth my time. When you are reviewing, you should be nailing down specific details (found in the book) rather than general concepts (found in the Becker flashcards).

On the other hand, if you want to create your own flashcards, that might be more effective. I believe that you will have a higher chance of recalling the information if you were the one to physically create the flashcard. Examining the information in the textbook and then physically writing it down can form a memory in your brain, which will further aid in your ability to recall the information. However, it is important to take into consideration the content of each exam and how time-efficiently you could translate that information into flashcards. The only exam I made flashcards for was BEC since there were ratios, mnemonics, and simple definitions to memorize. I personally think the content in the other exams would have taken too long to write out.

Even though I am a huge proponent of using every resource to your advantage, I never felt like I was missing out by skipping the flashcards. I think I reviewed more effectively and efficiently by simply reading the textbook and taking short practice tests. Like I said before, I know many people that love the Becker flashcards. I am going to leave it up to you to decide. I am just being 100% honest with you about my journey and what helped me score in the 90s.

Practice Tests
As some people swear by the flashcards, I swear by the practice tests! Practice tests in Becker allow you to choose which unit(s)

to review, as well as the number of MCQs and TBSs you want to be tested on. Practice tests are helpful to recall concepts from previous units as you continue to learn new information. Generally, I would take quick tests of 15 MCQs. Since I could take a 15 question test in about 10 minutes, I would do multiple of them per day. It is pretty hard to come up with an excuse of why you can't spend 10 minutes here and there to practice a few questions every day!

Maybe it's just me, but I found it much more manageable to do five 15 question tests rather than one 75 question test. Even though it would essentially be the same amount of questions, setting these smaller goals helped me feel less overwhelmed. I was also better able to learn from my mistakes since I would only have to analyze why I got a couple of questions wrong, if any, at a time.

I would complete these practice tests during every phase of studying to keep all of the units fresh in my memory. A common concern for candidates is forgetting information that you learned weeks ago. These practice tests will not only reassure you that you haven't forgotten everything, but they will also help you master the topics over time. Continual repetition has been proven to help with your long-term memory. By continually taking practice tests and being exposed to random questions every day, you are inevitably improving your brain's ability to recall the information.

Overall Advice
Take advantage of your study program. I know that time can be a constraint for some people; however, I never understood why candidates don't take advantage of resources that are right in front of them. If something is provided to help you learn, then use it. Like I said before, the only resource I chose not to use was the flashcards. However, do everything else! The lectures, skills practices, MCQs, TBSs, and practice tests are only there to help you. No matter what type of learning style you claim to have, there are

ways to see, hear, and write the content throughout Becker. To help the information stick, there is no reason why you shouldn't attempt everything provided to you! Becker has learned over the years how to perfect its material and how to teach it. Trust them. I think it is safe to say they know what they are doing.

*Note: I will discuss Becker's Simulated Exams and Final Review in my next chapter.

STUDY METHOD #3: REVIEW, REVIEW, REVIEW!!!

"Trust yourself, you know more than you think you do." – Benjamin Spock

Reviewing is HANDS DOWN the most CRUCIAL part of the studying process. It is inevitable to forget some of the things you learned while going through the modules the first time around. The review period is your chance to nail those details down before the exam.

After you get through all of the Becker "homework" for each unit, it is time to review! In my opinion, candidates do not take the review process seriously enough. After talking to my peers and reading online forums, it is apparent that many candidates do not know how to effectively review beyond using Becker's Final Review and Simulated Exams. They struggle with developing a study plan outside of what Becker recommends. In my opinion, everyone can complete the modules that Becker provides, but only the high-scoring test-takers will go above and beyond what they are "told" to do by a study program.

As I have mentioned before, I left about 3 weeks to review for each exam. This is a lot longer than what the average candidate takes. To give you some perspective, my peers took about 1-2 weeks. Anyways, I felt that I needed that extra time in order to feel confident about the material and to truly grasp the information. My peers would tell me, "there is no way to actually feel confident walking into an exam - there is just too much to know." However, with that extra review period, I would have to disagree. The extra week or so gave me the appropriate amount of time to get more comfortable with my weaker areas.

Becker's Final Review
The Final Review is a great resource to help reinforce the most heavily-tested topics. The Final Review is supplementary to Becker's main study program, and it consists of a summarized textbook, short online lectures, and additional MCQs and TBSs. I have heard many conflicting arguments on whether the Final Review is worth it or not. If your firm pays for it, then definitely take advantage of it! If not, I still think it is worth it for the following reasons: 1) it helps condense the material into a shorter amount of pages, which makes it easier to process the most important points, 2) it is easy to feel overwhelmed after finishing all of the Becker modules; the Final Review helps remind yourself that you know more than you think you do, and 3) you can never go wrong with additional MCQs and TBSs. All in all, all of the material really came together for me after doing the Final Review, and I highly recommend it.

I typically started Becker's Final Review immediately after finishing the Becker modules. I believe this timeline helped me grasp all of the information I had just learned over the past several weeks in only a matter of days. On average, I could get through the entire Final Review program in 3-4 days. Before even starting the program, I recommend creating a schedule of what you want to accomplish each day (sound familiar?). I would write down all of the lecture times on a piece of paper and then divide the total time up among 3-4 days. Each day, I would watch the lectures that

I had scheduled for the day, as well as completing the MCQs designated for those sections. The lectures are similar to the normal Becker ones, except shorter. Just as I recommended for the main Becker lectures, I suggest underlining and annotating just as the instructor does in the video. I guarantee that physically following along will help you process the information more than if you were to just sit and watch the videos.

In terms of the Final Review TBSs, I typically waited to complete them until later in the review process. For instance, if I was struggling with a certain area, I would go back to the Final Review program to see if there were any TBSs covering that topic. Most of the time, I did not complete every TBS that was provided. During the review process, I was more focused on nailing down details from the textbook and MCQs. That being said, don't ignore my advice from earlier... You should still do the TBSs provided in the normal modules. I just didn't find it necessary to complete all of the Final Review ones, as well.

Simulated Exams
Now that you have finished the normal Becker modules, as well as the Final Review, it is time to take a simulated exam! Becker offers 3 full-length simulated exams, and they are virtually identical to what the actual exam looks like. I found these to be extremely helpful for several reasons. First, because they mimic the actual exam, you will be much more comfortable on exam day by knowing what to expect. The format, timing, and content are all almost identical. Second, the simulated exams help you understand what your weakest topics are so that you can go back and review those concepts before the actual exam. The end of the exam gives you a breakdown of your score by unit, which helps identify which concepts you need to revisit. Last, but certainly not least, the simulated exams are a great way to review!

Since I would always leave about 3 weeks to review, and the Final Review program takes 3-4 days, I would typically try to take my first simulated exam with 2-2.5 weeks left before my test date. Prior to the first simulated exam, I chose not to review on my own yet; my only goal was to have the Becker modules and Becker Final Review completed. By doing it this way, I could see how well I understood the topics after only completing what Becker "told" me to do. Before the next simulated exams, I would try to master my weaker areas on my own by either reading the textbook or redoing MCQs and TBSs. I tried to take the second simulated exam with 1-1.5 weeks left before my test date and the third simulated exam about 3-4 days before my test date.

I advise you to take the simulated exams seriously and treat them like the actual exam. Find a quiet and enclosed room, turn off your phone, and don't access your study materials during the exam. I chose to take them seriously to get an accurate reflection of where I stood. Too many people take them with various distractions and then wonder why they scored in the 50s. If you take them seriously, you will be able to better understand the topics you need to "cram" and the topics you can just lightly review over the next couple weeks. On a side note, don't fret too much about the score Becker gives you. I don't think it is an accurate depiction of what you will get on the actual exam. For example, I scored a 70% on my first REG simulated exam and a 95% on the actual exam. On the other hand, I scored an 88% on my first FAR simulated exam and a 90% on the actual exam. So, I scored 25% higher on the actual REG exam and 2% higher on FAR... I know... it doesn't really make sense. Therefore, take your Becker score with a grain of salt and pay more attention to what units you scored higher or lower on.

Studying what you got wrong in the simulated exams is extremely beneficial. In the MCQ testlets, Becker provides helpful explanations for each problem describing why the answer is correct and why the other answer choices are incorrect. I recommend reading these explanations for every single question since you might have gotten an answer correct with an incorrect way of thinking. In fact, as I have mentioned before, write down your mistakes so that you are more likely to never make that same mistake again! Even if it is just on a scratch piece of paper, write down the accounting concept that you misunderstood. I guarantee you will be less inclined to answer that question wrong the next time you see it. When reviewing TBSs, I recommend watching the SkillMaster videos. I have mentioned these videos briefly before, but I think they are important enough to reiterate again. Becker's SkillMaster videos are videos taught by expert instructors about how to approach each TBS. Not only will you get more comfortable with the TBS topic, but you will also receive expert advice on how to approach various question formats. Like I did with the lectures, I watched the SkillMaster videos at a faster speed.

AICPA Sample Test
If you want to be 100% certain on how the exam is formatted (for those of you who don't believe me that it is almost identical to Becker's simulated exams), take the AICPA Sample Tests. On the AICPA website, you can find condensed sample tests, which utilize an online version of the real CPA exam software. Each sample test only provides 10 MCQs and 6 TBSs (except BEC, which includes 3 TBSs and 2 WCTs); however, you should take advantage of any opportunity to practice questions before your exam!

What to Review Once You "Finish" the Study Program
Let's say that you get to a point where you have done all the Becker modules, Final Review, and have taken at least one simulated exam. Now what? This is the million-dollar question (or should I say "passing all of the exams on the first try" question...). My point is that many candidates do not know what else to study once they have completed all of the tasks in the study program. However, that time in between the Becker modules and the exam date was hands-down my most crucial study period. That time allowed me to pinpoint my weaker areas and study them until I could nearly recite the textbook.

So what did I do to review? Honestly, it varied per exam. For example, BEC seemed to consist of a ton of smaller facts to memorize, such as ratios and key terms, so I made my own flashcards. FAR consisted of lots of calculations and journal entries, so I had a whole notebook of worked out problems and T accounts. REG is all about memorizing taxation rules and regulations and being able to apply them, so I practiced TBSs for hours on end. Lastly, AUD was just a ton of different information about various engagements and audit procedures, so I kept rereading the textbook to soak in as much information as possible. All in all, the common denominator for EVERY exam seemed to be rereading the textbook, taking quick 15 MCQ practice tests, reviewing my log of missed questions, and redoing MCQs and TBSs from the modules I felt less confident about.

I know… I am saying that this is the most crucial time to study; yet, I cannot outline an exact study plan for you… But, hear me out. Everyone struggles with different areas. Therefore, the concepts that I needed to spend hours understanding will not be the same as yours. My best advice is to turn your weaknesses into strengths. Master your weaker areas to the point where any topic that you are asked about on exam day is on an equal playing field in your brain. It is fairly common for candidates to be so scared about certain topics being asked that they spend more time worrying than actually perfecting their knowledge about those topics. Use your time wisely - it is completely up to you to determine how confident you want to feel on exam day.

STUDY METHOD #4: LEARN HOW TO APPROACH EXAM DAY

"By failing to prepare, you are preparing to fail." – Benjamin Franklin

The time has finally arrived - exam day! Ahh! A part of me loved getting closer to exam day because it meant that another test could be done; however, it can be nerve-racking! I don't know anyone that doesn't get nervous before a big exam, especially an exam known to be so difficult. My goal in this chapter is to help you feel a little bit less anxious when you walk into the testing center for the first time by outlining exactly what you can expect from Prometric and your exam.

Prometric Testing Center Tips

Prometric is the national standardized test taking center that administers the CPA exams. I never experienced any issues while testing at Prometric. From the check-in process to the exam itself, everything always ran smoothly.

I took all of my exams in the morning testing slot, which started at 8:30 AM. I am not necessarily a "morning person" on a daily basis, but I am the type who becomes one on exam days due to nerves. For my first exam, I had every intention of waking up extra early to cram because that is what I did before my college exams. However, I quickly realized when I opened my book that morning that there is no way to cram hundreds of pages of a CPA book. As I was flipping through all of the pages, I started psyching myself out by thinking I didn't remember anything. I quickly put the book away and never studied the morning before an exam again. My best advice is to eat a good breakfast and just relax. Keep in mind that you know more than you think you do. You prepared for this day for weeks. That being said, I could not imagine waiting until noon to take the exam... I think I would start doubting myself with all of that extra time to think. However, you know yourself best. Sign up for the time you think works best for you.

Before leaving your home, don't forget your NTS (Notice to Schedule)! You NEED this document printed in order to take your exam. You not only need it to check in, but you also need it because it has your launch code written on it. The launch code is essentially your password; you need to enter the 7-digit code in order to begin the exam. Also, Prometric requires you to bring 2 forms of ID. I only ever needed my driver's license, but it is better to be safe than sorry by bringing another form.

My NTS stated to arrive at the testing center approximately 30 minutes before my scheduled exam time. I always arrived 45 minutes early (at 7:45 AM) just to be safe. I would typically arrive just as the administrators were unlocking the doors. By arriving early, I rarely had to wait in line, and I could get started right away. The first administrator would check my ID, give me a form to read, show me to my locker, and provide me with 2 dry-erase sheets and 2 markers. I was instructed to write my initials and launch code (from my NTS) on each sheet. The second administrator would take my picture and fingerprints, as well as perform other security measures. All of this only took about 10-15 minutes, so I was typically able to start all of my exams about 30 minutes before my scheduled exam time.

After completing all of the security procedures, you are led to a designated cubicle to take your exam. I would definitely recommend wearing the noise-cancelling headphones provided on your desk. Even though nobody is necessarily talking, there are still those occasional coughs or other test-takers obnoxiously tapping their feet against the floor (*insert eye roll here*). Trust me - wear the headphones.

Timing Tips

As soon as you sit down at your desk, you will be required to enter your launch code onto the keyboard. You will then have 5 minutes to "accept" a policy statement and confidentiality agreement. I would take this time to quickly write out my timing strategy in the corner of my dry-erase sheet. However, be cautious of your time! If the 5 minute time limit is exceeded, the exam will terminate and cannot be restarted.

I covered my exact timing for each exam in the "exam structure" chapter. As a recap, all I would do is write, for example, "3:20, 2:40, 2:00, 1:00," in the corner of my dry-erase board. This meant that when the clock hit 3:20, I should be moving on to Testlet 2 (and so on...). I would cross out the respective times as I completed each testlet. Time management is SO important during the CPA exams.

Did I follow this schedule to the exact minute? Not exactly, but I was pretty close. If there was one MCQ that I knew I could figure out but it would push me to the 3:17 mark, then I would do it. I just made up the 3 minutes elsewhere. You never know when you will get more difficult questions; so, of course, the schedule could vary. BUT, I think writing down times kept me accountable and forced me to move on from testlets I wasn't making progress on. The worst idea would be to spend an extra 20 minutes on one TBS just because you think you could eventually figure it out. 20

minutes is valuable time that you could have spent perfecting other questions, which would have led you to a higher score in the long run. For all you know, that one TBS that you spent extra time on could have been a pretest question that doesn't even count toward your score...

There is only one standard break, in between the third and fourth testlets, where the clock actually stops for 15 minutes. I always took advantage of this break by using the restroom and drinking some water. Theoretically, you can take a break in between the other testlets; however, the clock will NOT stop running. Unless it's an emergency, I would recommend only taking the standard break so that you can fully utilize the entire 4 hours.

MCQ Tips

My first suggestion is to take a first pass at the MCQs as quickly as possible. I am not saying to fly through them without actually understanding the question. I am saying that if you are unsure of the answer after a minute or so of contemplating, then just select your "best guess," flag the question, and move on to the next one. As I have already mentioned, time-management is key for the CPA exams. Don't waste your time on questions that you are not making progress on. However, if you still have time before you are supposed to move on (according to your predetermined schedule written on your dry-erase sheet), and you have already gone through all of the questions at least once, go back to your flagged questions! The answer might come to you after looking at the question with a fresh set of eyes.

Not only will this strategy allow you to focus on the questions you know you can get right on the first go-around (and therefore increase your probability of getting more questions correct); but, it will also allow you to still have time at the end to attempt to solve the more difficult ones. Additionally, I guarantee it will help you with time-management. Trust me. Looking at the clock and realizing you still have 10 minutes left to double check your answers is SO much more reassuring than realizing you still need to answer 10+ MCQs in that amount of time. What if you really understood those last few MCQs but answered them incorrectly because you had to rush to move on? This is why you can't dilly-dally in the beginning of the testlet. Make sure to give every question a fair shot by not wasting time contemplating questions that you will never end up figuring out.

TBS Tips
Every TBS will be formatted differently, so it is hard to give a set of all-encompassing tips. However, in general, my main recommendation is to slowly read the question. Take the time to really understand what it is asking you to do. This may seem obvious, but from firsthand experience, it is easy to find yourself rushing through reading the question in order to get a head start on solving it... However, I began to learn that by slowing down and understanding the question, I could actually get the TBS done in a shorter amount of time since I wasn't constantly going back and rereading the main set of facts. For those TBSs that include several exhibits, truly understanding the question will also help you know exactly what facts and figures to look for in the attachments in order to help you solve the question being asked.

It is also important to note the tools and features offered in the exam software. For instance, there is a copy and paste tool, which can be used to paste into Excel, the calculator, or the response area. Keyboard shortcuts of Ctrl+C and Ctrl+V will definitely come in handy during the exam. Also, when you select text within an exhibit, a highlight tool will appear. I found the highlight tool to be extremely helpful during my TBSs. Since some attachments can be somewhat wordy, or consist of many different numbers (like a table where you only need one figure), the highlight tool allows you to highlight only the important information needed to solve the problem. The texts will remain highlighted even when you close the exhibit. Lastly, as I have mentioned before, Excel is available for every testlet (a normal version of Excel, that is; Becker's Excel is not reflective of what you will see on exam day). If you are dealing with many different numbers and calculations during a TBS, I definitely recommend opening Excel and solving the problem in there. Excel is a great way to organize and store your data, especially since the online calculator provided during the exam is so basic.

Last, but certainly not least, you will be given access to the Authoritative Literature (AL) for every TBS. I will cover this next, but just keep in mind that the AL can help you with more than you think...

Authoritative Literature (AL) Tips

You are guaranteed to be given one AL question as a TBS (except for BEC, which incorporates the writing portion instead). In my own words, an AL question means that you have to search through the appropriate accounting standards in order to find the correct reference to answer the question being asked. Honestly, I looked forward to these questions! During the exam, I typically found the correct answer within 5-10 minutes. Therefore, I was able to spend more time on other, more difficult, TBSs. Don't get me wrong - there were some difficult Becker practice questions where I could not, for the life of me, find the correct reference. This made me a little nervous that I would not find the correct reference during the actual exam. However, I never had an issue on exam day and was always confident in my answers to AL questions. My best advice would be to really perfect using the "Advanced Search" feature and getting solid at determining what keywords to use. Typically, the correct keywords will be used in the question itself, so I recommend trying those words first!

You may consider my advice about keywords to be obvious. However, my "not so obvious" advice deals with using the AL to your advantage OUTSIDE of the normal AL questions. I wish I could find a statistic about how many candidates do not realize you can use the standards to help you with other TBSs. Of course, using the AL does not make sense for every type of question. For instance, let's use the AUD exam as an example. The AL won't help you determine if a certain deficiency is a material weakness - you need to use your own judgment for this. However, let's say that you are provided a question dealing with the correct wording of an audit opinion. There are sample audit opinions given in the AL that you could look at... This isn't cheating! It's using your resources to your advantage! And surprisingly enough, most candidates do not even realize the usefulness of the resources directly in front of them.

Here's another example of how the AL was used to my advantage during FAR. I cannot say what my TBS dealt with (trust me... I even reached out to the AICPA to check for you guys). However, vaguely speaking, it was an accounting concept that had many different variables involved. I started to get overwhelmed with all of the different details the question was throwing at me. So, I started searching in the AL to see if I could find anything to help me out. And I did... right there in the implementation guidance of the FASB Codification was almost an exact replica of my TBS question (give or take a few variables and a timing difference). "Implementation Guidance and Illustrations" is Section 55 of each Subtopic. Essentially, the FASB Codification includes these sections to walk through specific accounting problems in order to help readers better understand certain principles. Little did I know that the exam software would include an illustration almost identical to my TBS. To this day, I still wonder if the AIPCA knew they did this... I kind of think they did in order to see who was intelligent enough to search through the AL to find it. Who knows... My point is that the AL can help you with more than just the designated AL question. Exam tip: if you are ever stuck during a TBS, try searching through the AL - you never know what you might find.

Written Communication Task (WCT) Tips
The BEC exam will consist of 3 WCTs. To recap, you will have to

read a scenario and respond to the respective party, whether that be in the form of a memo, letter, etc... The graders essentially want to test your ability to construct professional, business documents, as well as test your knowledge about various BEC concepts. That being said, the grading is not as black-and-white, as let's say, the MCQs. The tips that I will provide are an accumulation of the strategies I have read about while studying for this section. Of course, I do not exactly know how well I scored on these essays, so it is hard to determine what worked and what didn't work. However, the following advice is consistent among many different online forums.

Unless your grade is on the borderline of a 75, a computer will grade your WCTs. Therefore, construct your responses accordingly... use standard English, complete sentences, relevant terms, introduction, body, and conclusion paragraphs... got it? I would argue that it is almost more important to understand what the computer will scan for than actually knowing the "answer" to the question. For instance, let's say that you know nothing about the topic. You can work around that! As long as you are able to formulate a few well-written paragraphs with some keywords thrown in there... you still have a good chance of scoring well. One tip would be to read the scenario and then immediately start writing down keywords and thoughts that come to your mind about that topic onto your dry-erase sheet. This will not only help you gather your thoughts, but it will also be a helpful resource to glance down at as you are writing in case you get stuck or need another topic to discuss.

With a quick Google search, you can find various templates to follow when constructing a WCT. In addition, Becker has tons of sample questions and responses that you can look at. For the purpose of this book, I am not going to provide a sample outline because there are just so many ways to attempt an essay question. I recommend researching how to approach WCTs on your own because, quite honestly, there are several good websites that can outline how to construct your written responses better than I can. Plus, WCTs are only 15% of one exam. I would rather focus on tips that can help you with all of the exams.

Post-Exam Tips

Don't overthink it. That's the best advice I can give. Did I follow my own advice? Not exactly. There would be some nights where I could not fall asleep because I was overanalyzing how I answered a certain MCQ or TBS question. But... I can confidently say that it is not worth it to do this to yourself. There is no way to even guess what score you will receive, and most of the time, your score isn't even reflective of how you felt walking out of the exam. For example, I was really worried while walking out of BEC. Granted, I thought I knew enough to get a passing score, but I struggled with the TBSs I was given. I actually went over my budgeted times on the simulation testlets; therefore, I was crunched for time during the writing portion. I just didn't feel that great about it. On the flip side, I felt fairly confident while walking out of FAR and AUD. All that being said, I scored higher on BEC than I did on FAR and AUD. This is proof that there is no way to gauge your score purely off of your gut feelings. All in all, hang in there until scores are released. I know it's hard, but there is nothing you can do once you submit the exam.

STUDY METHOD #5: MINDSET MATTERS

"The way to get started is to quit talking and begin doing." – Walt Disney

I f I ended the book right here, I would be depriving you of some of my most important advice. Yeah... that's right. I haven't even covered the good stuff yet. You ready for it? Here it is - having the right mindset is even more important than your ability to retain information. That's it. That's the secret. You can study all you want, but if you do not have the right mindset, you are setting yourself up for failure. You have to be committed to the CPA exams. You have to be motivated and confident. Those 3 letters behind your name will not be handed to you. You have to want it!

What is motivating you to complete the CPA exams? Has it simply been a life-long goal of yours? Do you want to pass them all before you start work? Are you looking forward to the bonus your firm will provide once you pass them? Will those 3 letters behind your name give you a raise? Whatever the reasons are - keep them in mind throughout the entire process. If you have an end goal in mind, you are much more likely to buckle down and get the exams done as quick as possible. I cannot tell you how many times that I woke up in the morning not in the mood to study. But you know what? I reminded myself that I wanted to have all four exams passed before I started work in September. I had a goal. That goal kept me going every day for 7 months. What's your motivation?

Speaking of motivation, let's be real... my motivation went downhill as I completed each exam. By a lot. It became incredibly difficult to focus every day after studying for so many months. However, I just kept reminding myself of my goals (and how good it will feel when I am finished)! I knew that if I slacked during my last exam, I would regret it. Retaking it wouldn't have been the end of the world, but it would have delayed the entire process by at least a month. I know for a fact that if I was still studying come September when I started work, I would be extremely frustrated with myself knowing I had the opportunity to be finished and decided to procrastinate instead. In my opinion, you might as well put as much effort as possible into each exam to avoid extending the process any longer than you have to.

Finding internal motivation is obviously a key factor in passing the CPA exams; however, I also found myself being motivated from external sources like my fellow John Carroll classmates. John Carroll is known for its well-established accounting department; therefore, I was fortunate to get to know several bright accounting students throughout both my undergraduate and graduate education. A handful of accounting majors, like myself, decided to do the MBA program in order to reach 150 credits. Since many of us reached the credit requirement in December, I was certainly not the only one studying come January. In fact, I would be shocked if I didn't see someone I knew studying in the library on any given day. Anyways, I loved having a group of friends that were going through the same journey. Whether we talked about a specific accounting issue, how our exams went, or even how much studying sucks (venting is healthy, right?), it always felt reassuring knowing that somebody else can relate. I strongly believe that we found motivation through each other to keep going. My advice is this - find at least one other person you know studying for the exams, or at least someone who has been through the process before. This person will not only be able to help you with any questions and concerns you have about the exam, but I guarantee they will help keep you sane by sincerely understanding what you are going through.

I would like to add a side note about motivation. Obviously, it is incredibly important for you to stay motivated. If you lose your drive to study, you will not pass the exams. It is as simple as that. However, it is equally important to find a balance between working hard and recharging. If you study 24/7, you are guaranteed to burn out. You do not need to study all day, every day. In fact, your brain loses efficiency with sleep deprivation. It's not worth it! Don't make this process more stressful than it needs to be. Many people assume that I studied a crazy amount of time in order to score in the 90s. This is not true. I still took the time to see my friends and family, exercise, and go on a short vacation. I am not necessarily saying that you should say "yes" to every fun opportunity that comes your way. I am saying that there needs to be a balance. For instance, when I studied, I used my time wisely! When I sat down to review, I put 100% effort in so that I could afford to take those breaks (hint: shut off your phone...). Finding the perfect balance might take a little time, but once you find it, I guarantee your brain will be more alert while studying after you allow yourself those times to recharge.

Alright, I think I have covered enough about motivation. Let's talk about confidence now, shall we? I realize that saying to "be confident" is easier said than done. However, if you use my study methods and are exposed to the material in a variety of different ways, why shouldn't you feel confident? After putting in hundreds of hours into these exams, I think it is a logical assumption to say that you know more than you think you do. That being said, be confident going into the exams! I promise that being calm, cool, collected, and CONFIDENT while taking the exams will lead to higher scores and improved time-management. When you are overwhelmed and stressed, your mind will start thinking about failing instead of focusing on the exam right in front of you. Therefore, you will not think clearly about information you clearly know and have studied for weeks! Before you know it, you have lost track of time and have to start scrambling in order to move on to the next testlet. The phrase "self-fulfilling prophecy" immediately comes to mind when I think about this downward spiral. I am not trying to scare you. I am trying to get my point across that your mindset has a major role in dictating how well you do! Be confident and trust yourself. I am a firm believer that if you are confident, you will do a heck of a lot better on the CPA exams. Period.

GOOD LUCK!

"There is no substitute for hard work." – Thomas Edison

Whew! If you are still reading this, thank you for sticking around! I am hoping that you have learned some helpful tips on how to approach both the studying process and the exam itself. Again, my study methods might not work for everyone, but I felt obligated to share them with the world since they led me to scores in the 90s! I genuinely hope that my advice can help others succeed, too!

The process may seem never-ending, but I promise it will be worth it in the end. One last piece of advice: do it right the first time so you won't have to do it again! This mentality may seem self-explanatory; but, only those who truly believe it will succeed...

From the bottom of my heart, I wish you the best of luck on your CPA journey. You've got this!

Made in United States
Orlando, FL
16 May 2023

33206366R00031